CW00840010

Mark T

Quotes & Facts

By Blago Kirov

First Edition

Translated by Krasi Vasileva

*****

Mark Twain: Quotes & Facts
*****

Foreword

"The human race has only one really effective weapon and that is laughter."

This book is an anthology of 233 quotes from Mark Twain and selected facts about Mark Twain. It grants his reflections on subjects ranging from Writing and Art of Life to Stupidity and God; in addition, the book shows the personality of Mark Twain into a different than legend, more human light:

Mark Twain was born two weeks after Halley's Comet appeared in its closest approach to the Earth.
Mark Twain stood 5 feet 8 1/2 inches tall.
Mark Twain belonged to the Freemasons.
Mark Twain wrote a total of 28 books along with essays, articles, and short stories.
There are no direct heirs to Mark Twain surviving today.
Mark Twain did not graduate elementary school.
Mark Twain was a close friend of Dr. Nikola Tesla.
Mark Twain first donned his famous white suit in 1906, when he appeared before Congress to testify about copyright law.
Mark Twain was born Samuel Langhorne Clemens on November 30, 1835 in the town of Florida, Missouri.

"Writing is easy. All you have to do is cross out the wrong words."
"The human race has only one really effective weapon and that is laughter."
"The lack of money is the root of all evil."
"It's not the size of the dog in the fight; it's the size of the fight in the dog."
"A banker is a fellow who lends you his umbrella when the sun is shining, but wants it back the minute it begins to rain."

"For business reasons, I must preserve the outward signs of sanity."

"Go to heaven for the climate and hell for the company."

"Jim said that bees won't sting idiots, but I didn't believe that, because I tried them lots of times myself and they wouldn't sting me."

"If you tell the truth, you don't have to remember anything."

Some Facts about Mark Twain

Mark Twain was born two weeks after Halley's Comet appeared in its closest approach to the Earth.

Mark Twain stood 5 feet 8 1/2 inches tall.

Mark Twain belonged to the Freemasons.

Mark Twain wrote a total of 28 books along with essays, articles, and short stories.

There are no direct heirs to Mark Twain surviving today.

Mark Twain did not graduate elementary school.

Mark Twain was a close friend of Dr. Nikola Tesla.

Mark Twain first donned his famous white suit in 1906, when he appeared before Congress to testify about copyright law.

Mark Twain was born Samuel Langhorne Clemens on November 30, 1835 in the town of Florida, Missouri.

His father was John Marshall Clemens, who worked as a Tennessee country merchant.

Mark Twain's father died of pneumonia when Mark was 12.

From the ages of 18 to 22 Mark Twain worked as a printer, traveling from Missouri to New York, Cincinnati, Philadelphia and St. Louis.

Mark Twain became a steamboat pilot in 1859 after befriending Horace E. Biby, a steamboat pilot, and memorizing over 2000 miles of riverbed.

From his experience as a licensed river pilot, Samuel Langhorne Clemens chose the pen name by which he his best known - Mark Twain. The term "mark twain" means it is safe to sail because the water's depth is two fathoms, or 12 feet. "Mark one" is six feet, "mark three" is 18 feet, and "mark four" is 24 feet.

Other pseudonyms Mark Twain used as a writer were Thomas Jefferson Snodgrass, W. Epaminondas Adrastus Blab, Sergeant Fathom, and Rambler.

An article written in 1863 for the Virginia City Territorial Enterprise was the first published piece to use the Twain pseudonym.

His first book, "The Innocents Abroad", was published in 1869.

"The Adventures of Huckleberry Finn", published in 1885, has been called the first "Great American Novel."

During his trip to the Mediterranean, Mark Twain met his future brother-in-law who, in turn, introduced him to his future wife, Olivia Langdon.

Mark Twain was married to Olivia Langdon for 34 years and they had four children: Susy, Langdon, Clara and Jean Clemens.

His son Langdon died of diphtheria at the age of 19 months.

His daughter Suzy and Jean both died in their 20s.

His surviving daughter, Clara, lived until 1962 and had a daughter of her own who died childless

Mark Twain's book "Tom Sawyer" (1876) was the first novel ever to be written on a typewriter.

To pay off debts accumulated as a result of failed business ventures, Mark Twain toured the world as a lecturer, publishing his experiences in "Following the Equator" (1897).

Mark Twain went bankrupt in 1894.

Mark Twain loved cats and wanted them around him all the time.

During the last years of his life, Mark Twain was the vice-president of the American Anti-Imperialist League.

Mark Twain predicts in 1909: "I came in with Halley's Comet in 1835. It is coming again next year, and I expect to go out with it. It will be the greatest disappointment of my life if I don't go out with Halley's Comet." As he predicted, he died 74 years old on April 21, 1910, of a heart attack, the day after Halley's Comet made its closest pass.

During the American Civil War, Mark Twain formed a confederate militia group known as the Marion Rangers, which disbanded after two weeks.

In 1907, Mark Twain received a Doctorate in Letters from Oxford University.

Mark Twain often made bad investments, which resulted in serious financial problems.

Mark Twain dined with Germany's Kaiser Wilhelm II in 1892 while traveling through Europe.

Mark Twain was very interested in parapsychology.

Mark Twain met Harriet Beecher Stowe in 1868.

Mark Twain ordered all his manuscripts burned when he died.

Mark Twain loved to write in bed.

Bermuda was the last foreign locale Mark Twain visited before he died.

Mark Twain claimed to be the first person in New England to have had a telephone for private use.

William Faulkner called Mark Twain "the father of American literature".

Mark Twain gave his cats inventive names such as Bambino, Famine, Pestilence, Satan, Sin, Sour Mash, and Stray Kit.

One of Mark Twain's closest friends was Henry Rogers.

Mark Twain was a redhead in his youth.

Mark Twain died of a heart attack.

Mark Twain first used the fingerprinting evidence to solve a crime in one of his fictional novels, "Life on the Mississippi".

The character of Huckleberry Finn was modeled after Mark Twain's boyhood friend Tom Blankenship. "

Mark Twain was a inventor. Three of his inventions were patented: an automatically self-adjusting vest strap, a history game meant for improving memory, and a self-pasting scrapbook--the only one ever to make him any money.

In 1856, Mark Twain moved to Cincinnati, where he hatched a plan to travel to South America to collect coca leaves.

Mark Twain was a passenger on the first "luxury cruise" to Europe and the Holy Land, and related the party's misadventures in letters to the New York Tribune and the Herald.

Mark Twain was a successful lecturer, generating money and fame via speaking tours throughout the United States and Europe.

Mark Twain suffered from color blindness.

One of Mark Twain's biggest literary influences was The Arabian Nights.

Mark Twain greatly admired the poet Robert Browning he later met in 1873.

His Words

"Writing is easy. All you have to do is cross out the wrong words."

"The human race has only one really effective weapon and that is laughter."

"The lack of money is the root of all evil."

"It's not the size of the dog in the fight; it's the size of the fight in the dog."

"A banker is a fellow who lends you his umbrella when the sun is shining, but wants it back the minute it begins to rain."

"For business reasons, I must preserve the outward signs of sanity."

"Go to heaven for the climate and hell for the company."

"Jim said that bees won't sting idiots, but I didn't believe that, because I tried them lots of times myself and they wouldn't sting me."

"If you tell the truth, you don't have to remember anything."

"A big leather-bound volume makes an ideal razor strap. A thing book is useful to stick under a table with a broken caster to steady it. A large, flat atlas can be used to cover a window with a broken pane. And a thick, old-fashioned heavy book with a clasp is the finest thing in the world to throw at a noisy cat."

"A clear conscience is the sure sign of a bad memory."

"A gentleman is someone who knows how to play the banjo and doesn't."

"A half-truth is the most cowardly of lies."

"A home without a cat — and a well-fed, well-petted and properly revered cat — may be a perfect home, perhaps, but how can it prove title?"

"A lie can travel half way around the world while the truth is putting on its shoes."

"A man cannot be comfortable without his own approval."

"A man is accepted into a church for what he believes and he is turned out for what he knows."

"A man is never more truthful than when he acknowledges himself a liar."

"A man who is not born with the novel-writing gift has a troublesome time of it when he tries to build a novel. I know this from experience. He has no clear idea of his story; in fact he has no story. He merely has some people in his mind, and an incident or two, also a locality, and he trusts he can plunge those people into those incidents with interesting results. So he goes to work. To write a novel? No - that is a thought which comes later; in the beginning he is only proposing to tell a little tale, a very little tale, a six-page tale. But as it is a tale which he is not acquainted with, and can only find out what it is by listening as it goes along telling itself, it is more than apt to go on and on and on till it spreads itself into a book. I know about this, because it has happened to me so many times."

"A man's character may be learned from the adjectives which he habitually uses in conversation."

"A person that started in to carry a cat home by the tail was getting knowledge that was always going to be useful to him, and weren't ever going to grow dim or doubtful."

"A successful book is not made of what is in it, but what is left out of it."

"Action speaks louder than words but not nearly as often."

"Adam was but human—this explains it all. He did not want the apple for the apple's sake; he wanted it only because it was forbidden. The mistake was in not forbidding the serpent; then he would have eaten the serpent."

"After all these years, I see that I was mistaken about Eve in the beginning; it is better to live outside the Garden with her than inside it without her."
"Against the assault of laughter, nothing can stand."
"All right, then, I'll go to hell."

"All you need in this life is ignorance and confidence; then success is sure."

"Always acknowledge a fault. This will throw those in authority off their guard and give you an opportunity to commit more."

"Always do what is right. It will gratify half of mankind and astound the other."

"Anger is an acid that can do more harm to the vessel in which it is stored than to anything on which it is poured."

"Any emotion, if it is sincere, is involuntary."

"April 1. This is the day upon which we are reminded of what we are on the other three hundred and sixty-four."

"Be careful about reading health books. You may die of a misprint."

"Be good and you will be lonesome."

"Be respectful to your superiors, if you have any."

"Books are for people who wish they were somewhere else."

"But who prays for Satan? Who, in eighteen centuries, has had the common humanity to pray for the one sinner that needed it most?"

"Censorship is telling a man he can't have a steak just because a baby can't chew it."

"Civilization is a limitless multiplication of unnecessary necessaries."

"Classic' - a book which people praise and don't read."

"Clothes make the man. Naked people have little or no influence on society."

"Courage is resistance to fear, mastery of fear - not absence of fear."

"December is the toughest month of the year. Others are July, January, September, April, November, May, March, June, October, August, and February."

"Distance lends enchantment to the view."

"Do something everyday that you don't want to do; this is the golden rule for acquiring the habit of doing your duty without pain."

"Don't go around saying the world owes you a living. The world owes you nothing. It was here first."

"Don't part with your illusions. When they are gone you may still exist, but you have ceased to live."

"Don't say the old lady screamed. Bring her on and let her scream."

"Don't wake up a woman in love. Let her dream, so that she does not weep when she returns to her bitter reality"

"Drag your thoughts away from your troubles...by the ears, by the heels, or any other way you can manage it."

"Eat a live frog first thing in the morning and nothing worse will happen to you the rest of the day."

"Education consists mainly of what we have unlearned."

"Education: that which reveals to the wise, and conceals from the stupid, the vast limits of their knowledge."

"Education: the path from cocky ignorance to miserable uncertainty."

"Every person is a book, each year a chapter,"

"Every time you stop a school, you will have to build a jail. What you gain at one end you lose at the other. It's like feeding a dog on his own tail. It won't fatten the dog."

"Everyone is a moon, and has a dark side which he never shows to anybody."

"Everyone talks about the weather, but no one does anything about it."

"Explaining humor is a lot like dissecting a frog, you learn a lot in the process, but in the end you kill it."

"Facts are stubborn things, but statistics are pliable."

"Familiarity breeds contempt and children."

"Few things are harder to put up with than the annoyance of a good example."

"Forgiveness is the fragrance that the violet sheds on the heel that has crushed it."

"Get your facts first, and then you can distort them as much as you please."

"Giving up smoking is the easiest thing in the world. I know because I've done it thousands of times."

"God created war so that Americans would learn geography."

"Good friends, good books, and a sleepy conscience: this is the ideal life."

"Good judgment is the result of experience and experience the result of bad judgment."

"Great people are those who make others feel that they, too, can become great."

"Grief can take care of itself, but to get the full value of joy you must have somebody to divide it with."

"Habit is habit, and not to be flung out of the window by any man, but coaxed down-stairs one step at a time."

"He had had much experience of physicians, and said 'the only way to keep your health is to eat what you don't want, drink what you don't like, and do what you'd druther not'."

"He who asks is a fool for five minutes, but he who does not ask remains a fool forever."

"Heaven goes by favor. If it went by merit, you would stay out and your dog would go in."

"History doesn't repeat itself, but it does rhyme."

"Honesty: The best of all the lost arts."

"Human beings can be awful cruel to one another."

"Humor is mankind's greatest blessing."

"I always take Scotch whiskey at night as a preventive of toothache. I have never had the toothache; and what is more, I never intend to have it."

"I am an old man and have known a great many troubles, but most of them have never happened."

"I can last two months on a good compliment."

"I can teach anybody how to get what they want out of life. The problem is that I can't find anybody who can tell me what they want."

"I did not attend his funeral, but I sent a nice letter saying I approved of it."

"I didn't have time to write a short letter, so I wrote a long one instead."

"I do not fear death. I had been dead for billions and billions of years before I was born, and had not suffered the slightest inconvenience from it."

"I have a higher and grander standard of principle than George Washington. He could not lie; I can, but I won't."

"I have found out that there aren't no surer way to find out whether you like people or hate them than to travel with them."

"I have never let my schooling interfere with my education."

"I haven't any right to criticize books, and I don't do it except when I hate them. I often want to criticize Jane Austen, but her books madden me so that I can't conceal my frenzy from the reader; and therefore I have to stop every time I begin. Every time I read Pride and Prejudice I want to dig her up and beat her over the skull with her own shin-bone."

"I know the look of an apple that is roasting and sizzling on the hearth on a winter's evening, and I know the comfort that comes of eating it hot, along with some sugar and a drench of cream... I know how the nuts taken in conjunction with winter apples, cider, and doughnuts, make old people's tales and old jokes sound fresh and crisp and enchanting."

"I must have a prodigious amount of mind; it takes me as much as a week, sometimes, to make it up!"

"I notice that you use plain, simple language, short words and brief sentences. That is the way to write English — it is the modern way and the best way. Stick to it; don't let fluff and flowers and verbosity creep in. When you catch an adjective, kill it. No, I don't mean utterly, but kill most of them — then the rest will be valuable. They weaken when they are close together. They give strength when they are wide apart. An adjective habit, or a wordy, diffuse, flowery habit, once fastened upon a person, is as hard to get rid of as any other vice."

"I said there was nothing so convincing to an Indian as a general massacre. If he could not approve of the massacre, I said the next surest thing for an Indian was soap and education. Soap and education are not as sudden as a massacre, but they are more deadly in the long run; because a half-massacred Indian may recover, but if you educate him and wash him, it is bound to finish him some time or other."

"I take my only exercise acting as a pallbearer at the funerals of my friends who exercise regularly."

"I thoroughly disapprove of duels. If a man should challenge me, I would take him kindly and forgivingly by the hand and lead him to a quiet place and kill him."

"I was gratified to be able to answer promptly, and I did. I said I didn't know."

"I was sorry to have my name mentioned as one of the great authors, because they have a sad habit of dying off. Chaucer is dead, Spencer is dead, so is Milton, so is Shakespeare, and I'm not feeling so well myself."

"If animals could speak, the dog would be a blundering outspoken fellow; but the cat would have the rare grace of never saying a word too much."

"If books are not good company, where shall I find it?"

"If Christ were here there is one thing he would not be—a Christian."

"If voting made any difference they wouldn't let us do it."

"If we would learn what the human race really is at bottom, we need only observe it in election times."

"If you don't read the newspaper, you're uninformed. If you read the newspaper, you're mist informed."

"If you pick up a starving dog and make him prosperous he will not bite you. This is the principal difference between a dog and man."

"Ignorant people think it is the noise which fighting cats make that is so aggravating, but it ain't so; it is the sickening grammar that they use."

"In a good bookroom you feel in some mysterious way that you are absorbing the wisdom contained in all the books through your skin, without even opening them."

"In Paris they just simply opened their eyes and stared when we spoke to them in French! We never did succeed in making those idiots understand their own language."

"In religion and politics people's beliefs and convictions are in almost every case gotten at second-hand, and without examination, from authorities who have not themselves examined the questions at issue but have taken them at second-hand from other non-examiners, whose opinions about them were not worth a brass farthing."

"In the beginning of a change the patriot is a scarce man, and brave, and hated and scorned. When his cause succeeds, the timid join him, for then it costs nothing to be a patriot."

"In the first place God made idiots. This was for practice. Then he made school boards."

"It could probably be shown by facts and figures that there is no distinctly Native American criminal class except Congress."
"It is better to deserve honors and not have them than to have them and not deserve them."

"It is by the goodness of god that in our country we have those 3 unspeakably precious things: freedom of speech, freedom of conscience, and the prudence never to practice either of them."

"It is curious that physical courage should be so common in the world and moral courage so rare."

"It is easier to stay out than to get out."

"It takes your enemy and your friend, working together, to hurt you to the heart: the one to slander you and the other to get the news to you."

"It usually takes me two or three days to prepare an impromptu speech."

"It's better to keep your mouth shut and appear stupid than open it and remove all doubt"

"It's easier to fool people than to convince them that they have been fooled."

"It's easy to make friends, but hard to get rid of them."

"It's not what you don't know that kills you, it's what you know for sure that aren't true."

"I've had a lot of worries in my life, most of which never happened."

"Just because you're taught that something's right and everyone believes it's right, it don't make it right."

"Just the omission of Jane Austen's books alone would make a fairly good library out of a library that hadn't a book in it."

"Keep away from people who try to belittle your ambitions. Small people always do that, but the really great make you feel that you, too, can become great."

"Kindness is a language which the deaf can hear and the blind can see."

"Let us be thankful for the fools. But for them the rest of us could not succeed. "

"Let us consider that we are all partially insane. It will explain us to each other; it will unriddle many riddles; it will make clear and simple many things which are involved in haunting and harassing difficulties and obscurities now."

"Life does not consist mainly, or even largely, of facts or happenings. It consists mainly of the storm of thoughts that is forever flowing through one's head."

"Life is short, break the Rules, forgive quickly, and kiss slowly, love truly, laugh uncontrollably and never regret anything. That makes you smile."

"Man has imagined a heaven, and has left entirely out of it the supreme of all his delights...sexual intercourse! His heaven is like himself: strange, interesting, astonishing, grotesque. I give you my word; it has not a single feature in it that he actually values."

"Man is the only animal that blushes. Or needs to."

"There are three things men can do with women: love them, suffer them, or turn them into literature."

"Let us live so that when we come to die even the undertaker will be sorry."

"I've lived through some terrible things in my life, some of which actually happened."

"Man is the Reasoning Animal. Such is the claim. I think it is open to dispute. Indeed, my experiments have proven to me that he is the Unreasoning Animal... In truth, man is incurably foolish. Simple things which other animals easily learn, he is incapable of learning. Among my experiments was this. In an hour I taught a cat and a dog to be friends. I put them in a cage. In another hour I taught them to be friends with a rabbit. In the course of two days I was able to add a fox, a goose, a squirrel and some doves. Finally a monkey. They lived together in peace; even affectionately. Next, in another cage I confined an Irish Catholic from Tipperary, and as soon as he seemed tame I added a Scotch Presbyterian from Aberdeen. Next a Turk from Constantinople; a Greek Christian from Crete; an Armenian; a Methodist from the wilds of Arkansas; a Buddhist from China; a Brahman from Benares. Finally, a Salvation Army Colonel from Wapping. Then I stayed away for two whole days. When I came back to note results, the cage of Higher Animals was all right, but in the other there was but a chaos of gory odds and ends of turbans and fezzes and plaids and bones and flesh-- not a specimen left alive. These Reasoning Animals had disagreed on a theological detail and carried the matter to a Higher Court."

"Man was made at the end of the week's work when God was tired."

"Many public-school children seem to know only two dates—1492 and 4th of July; and as a rule they don't know what happened on either occasion."

"Most people are bothered by those passages of Scripture they do not understand, but the passages that bother me are those I do understand."

"Most writers regard the truth as their most valuable possession, and therefore are economical in its use."

"My books are water; those of the great geniuses are wine. Everybody drinks water."

"Name the greatest of all inventors. Accident."

"Never allow someone to be your priority while allowing yourself to be their option."

"Never argue with a fool, onlookers may not be able to tell the difference."

"Never argue with stupid people, they will drag you down to their level and then beat you with experience."

"Never put off till tomorrow what may be done day after tomorrow just as well".

"Never tell the truth to people who are not worthy of it."

"New Orleans food is as delicious as the less criminal forms of sin."

"No man's life, liberty, or property is safe while the legislature is in session."

"Noise proves nothing. Often a hen who has laid an egg cackles as if she had laid an asteroid."

"Now and then we had a hope that if we lived and were good, God would permit us to be pirates."

"Obscurity and a competence — that is the life that is best worth living."

"Of all God's creatures, there is only one that cannot be made slave of the leash. That one is the cat. If man could be crossed with the cat it would improve the man, but it would deteriorate the cat."

"Of all the animals, man is the only one that is cruel. He is the only one that inflicts pain for the pleasure of doing it."

"Often it does seem such a pity that Noah and his party did not miss the boat."

"One of the most striking differences between a cat and a lie is that a cat has only nine lives."

"Out of all the things I have lost, I miss my mind the most."

"Part of the secret of success in life is to eat what you like and let the food fight it out inside."

"Patriotism is supporting your country all the time and your government when it deserves it."

"Peace by persuasion has a pleasant sound, but I think we should not be able to work it. We should have to tame the human race first, and history seems to show that that cannot be done."

"Plain question and plain answer make the shortest road out of most perplexities."

"Politicians and diapers must be changed often, and for the same reason."

"Reader, suppose you were an idiot. And suppose you were a member of Congress. But I repeat myself."

"Reality can be beaten with enough imagination."

"Sanity and happiness are an impossible combination."

"She remained both girl and woman to the last day of her life. Under a grave and gentle exterior burned inextinguishable fires of sympathy, energy, devotion, enthusiasm, and absolutely limitless affection."

"Sometimes I wonder whether the world is being run by smart people who are putting us on or by imbeciles who really mean it."

"Substitute 'damn' every time you're inclined to write 'very;' your editor will delete it and the writing will be just as it should be."

"That is just the way with some people. They get down on a thing when they don't know nothing about it."

"The best way to cheer yourself is to try to cheer someone else up."

"The Bible has noble poetry in it... and some good morals and a wealth of obscenity, and upwards of a thousand lies."

"The common eye sees only the outside of things, and judges by that, but the seeing eye pierces through and reads the heart and the soul, finding there capacities which the outside didn't indicate or promise, and which the other kind of eye couldn't detect."

"The difference between the right word and the almost right word is the difference between lightning and a lightning bug."

"The dog is a gentleman; I hope to go to his heaven not man's."

"The easy confidence with which I know another man's religion is folly teaches me to suspect that my own is also."

"The fact that man knows right from wrong proves his intellectual superiority to the other creatures; but the fact that he can do wrong proves his moral inferiority to any creatures that cannot."

"The fear of death follows from the fear of life. A man who lives fully is prepared to die at any time."

"The government is merely a servant merely a temporary servant; it cannot be its prerogative to determine what is right and what is wrong, and decide who is a patriot and who isn't. Its function is to obey orders, not originate them."

"The man who does not read has no advantage over the man who cannot read."

"The man who is a pessimist before 48 knows too much; if he is an optimist after it he knows too little."

"The most interesting information come from children, for they tell all they know and then stop."

"The older I get, the more clearly I remember things that never happened."

"The only difference between a tax man and a taxidermist is that the taxidermist leaves the skin."

"The radical of one century is the conservative of the next. The radical invents the views. When he has worn them out, the conservative adopt."

"The reports of my death are greatly exaggerated."

"The right word may be effective, but no word was ever as effective as a rightly timed pause."

"The secret source of humor is not joy but sorrow; there is no humor in heaven."

"The secret to getting ahead is getting started."

"The so-called Christian nations are the most enlightened and progressive ... but in spite of their religion, not because of it. The Church has opposed every innovation and discovery from the day of Galileo down to our own time, when the use of anesthetic in childbirth was regarded as a sin because it avoided the biblical curse pronounced against Eve. And every step in astronomy and geology ever taken has been opposed by bigotry and superstition. The Greeks surpassed us in artistic culture and in architecture five hundred years before Christian religion was born."

"The trouble is not in dying for a friend, but in finding a friend worth dying for."

"The two most important days in your life are the day you are born and the day you find out why."

"The worst loneliness is to not be comfortable with yourself."

"There are many humorous things in the world; among them, the white man's notion that he is less savage than the other savages."

"There are several good protections against temptations, but the surest is cowardice."

"There are those who scoff at the schoolboy, calling him frivolous and shallow: Yet it was the schoolboy who said 'Faith is believing what you know aren't so'."

"There has never been a just [war], never an honorable one--on the part of the instigator of the war. I can see a million years ahead, and this rule will never change in so many as half a dozen instances. The loud little handful--as usual--will shout for the war. The pulpit will--warily and cautiously--object--at first; the great, big, dull bulk of the nation will rub its sleepy eyes and try to make out why there should be a war, and will say, earnestly and indignantly, 'It is unjust and dishonorable, and there is no necessity for it.' Then the handful will shout louder. A few fair men on the other side will argue and reason against the war with speech and pen, and at first will have a hearing and be applauded; but it will not last long; those others will outshoot them, and presently the anti-war audiences will thin out and lose popularity. Before long you will see this curious thing: the speakers stoned from the platform, and free speech strangled by hordes of furious men who in their secret hearts are still at one with those stoned speakers--as earlier--but do not dare say so. And now the whole nation--pulpit and all--will take up the war-cry, and shout itself hoarse, and mob any honest man who ventures to open his mouth; and presently such mouths will cease to open. Next the statesmen will invent cheap lies, putting the blame upon the nation that is attacked, and every man will be glad of those conscience-soothing falsities, and will diligently study them, and refuse to examine any refutations of them; and thus he will by and by convince himself the war is just, and will thank God for the better sleep he enjoys after this process of grotesque self-deception."

"There is a charm about the forbidden that makes it unspeakably desirable."

"There is no sadder sight than a young pessimist, except an old optimist."

"There is nothing so annoying as having two people talking when you're busy interrupting."

"There was never yet an uninteresting life. Such a thing is an impossibility. Inside of the dullest exterior there is a drama, a comedy, and a tragedy."

"There's one way to find out if a man is honest: ask him; if he says yes, you know he's crooked."

"Thunder is good, thunder is impressive; but it is lightening that does the work."

"To do good is noble. To tell others to do good is even nobler and much less trouble."

"To get the full value of joy you must have someone to divide it with."

"Too much of anything is bad, but too much good whiskey is barely enough."

"Training is everything. The peach was once a bitter almond; cauliflower is nothing but cabbage with a college education."

"Travel is fatal to prejudice, bigotry, and narrow-mindedness, and many of our people need it sorely on these accounts. Broad, wholesome, charitable views of men and things cannot be acquired by vegetating in one little corner of the earth all one's lifetime."

"Truth is stranger than fiction, but it is because Fiction is obliged to stick to possibilities; Truth isn't."

"Unconsciously we all have a standard by which we measure other men, and if we examine closely we find that this standard is a very simple one, and is this: we admire them, we envy them, for great qualities we ourselves lack. Hero worship consists in just that. Our heroes are men who do things which we recognize, with regret, and sometimes with a secret shame, that we cannot do. We find not much in ourselves to admire, we are always privately wanting to be like somebody else. If everybody was satisfied with himself, there would be no heroes."

"Under certain circumstances, profanity provides a relief denied even to prayer."

"We may not pay Satan reverence, for that would be indiscreet, but we can at least respect his talents."

"What a wee little part of a person's life are his acts and his words! His real life is led in his head, and is known to none but himself. All day long, the mill of his brain is grinding, and his thoughts, not those of other things, are his history. These are his life, and they are not written. Everyday would make a whole book of 80,000 words -- 365 books a year. Biographies are but the clothes and buttons of the man -- the biography of the man himself cannot be written."

"What is joy without sorrow? What is success without failure? What is a win without a loss? What is health without illness? You have to experience each if you are to appreciate the other. There is always going to be suffering. it's how you look at your suffering, how you deal with it, that will define you."

"What is Man? Man is a noisome bacillus whom Our Heavenly Father created because he was disappointed in the monkey."

"What would men be without women? Scarce, sir... mighty scarce."

"When angry, count four. When very angry, swear."

"When I am king they shall not have bread and shelter only, but also teachings out of books, for a full belly is little worth where the mind is starved."
"When I was a boy of 14, my father was so ignorant I could hardly stand to have the old man around. But when I got to be 21, I was astonished at how much the old man had learned in seven years."

"When I was younger, I could remember anything, whether it had happened or not; but my faculties are decaying now and soon I shall be so I cannot remember any but the things that never happened. It is sad to go to pieces like this but we all have to do it."

"When people do not respect us we are sharply offended; yet deep down in his private heart no man much respects himself."

"When red-headed people are above a certain social grade their hair is auburn."

"When we remember we are all mad, the mysteries disappear and life stands explained."

"When you fish for love, bait with your heart, not your brain."

"Whenever you find yourself on the side of the majority, it is time to pause and reflect."

"Whiskey is for drinking; water is for fighting over."

"Whosesoever she was, there was Eden."

"Why do you sit there looking like an envelope without any address on it?"

"Worrying is like paying a debt you don't owe."

"Wrinkles should merely indicate where the smiles have been."

"Write what you know."

"Write without pay until somebody offers to pay."

"You believe in a book that has talking animals, wizards, witches, demons, sticks turning into snakes, burning bushes, food falling from the sky, people walking on water, and all sorts of magical, absurd and primitive stories and you say that we are the ones that need help?"

"You can't depend on your eyes when your imagination is out of focus."

Printed in Great Britain
by Amazon

42571085R00030